P9-EGN-184

Jimi's Book of Japanese

A Motivating Method to Learn Japanese™ (Hiragana)

omnimedia™

Jimi's Book of Japanese: A Motivating Method to Learn Japanese™ (Hiragana)

Published in the United States by PB&J Omnimedia™
A division of Takahashi & Black™

Design and layout copyright ©2002, ©2005 by Yumie Toka
Illustrations copyright ©2002, ©2005 by Yumie Toka
Text copyright ©2002, ©2005 by Peter X. Takahashi

Second printing 2005

All rights reserved. No part of this book may be reproduced, stored in a retrieval system, or transmitted in any form or by any means, electronic, photocopying, recording or otherwise, without prior written permission from the publisher.

PB&J Omnimedia™ Triple Bubble Learning System™, characters, names, logos and indicia are trademarks and/or registered trademarks of PB&J Omnimedia™ and Takahashi & Black™. For licensing information, please contact us.

Library of Congress Control Number 2002111509

ISBN 0-9723247-0-4

Printed in Singapore

Typeset in Adobe Frutiger and Osaka

A PB&J Omnimedia™ book

10   9   8   7   6   5   4   3   2

PB&J Omnimedia™ products are available at special discounts for bulk purchases in the United States by corporations, institutions, and people named Mojo. For international discount programs and other information, please contact us.

PB&J Omnimedia™
www.pbjomnimedia.com

Jimi's Book of Japanese
A Motivating Method to Learn Japanese™ (Hiragana)

Peter X. Takahashi
Illustrations by Yumie Toka

pb&j
omnimedia™

About *kana*

Instead of an alphabet, Japanese uses *kana*. Each *kana* represents a syllable. There are two kinds of *kana*: *hiragana* and *katakana*. *Hiragana* is used for the traditional sounds of Japanese. *Katakana* is used for words Japanese has borrowed from other languages. Both *kana* sets are what you use when you first learn Japanese.

These two sets are mixed with Chinese characters, called *kanji*. Each *kanji* represents a word or idea and may be pronounced several different ways depending on its use. There are thousands of *kanji*. It takes many years to learn them so it is best to master *kana* while learning a few *kanji* at a time.

There are many ways to transliterate *kana*. All *kana* in this book are matched with *romaji*, a script used to teach Japanese to foreigners. Below is a guide to help you pronounce *romaji*.

About pronunciation
Vowels

Japanese has five vowel sounds and it takes a bit of practice to learn them. On every page, you'll find a pronunciation key. Wherever you see the key, say:

"a"	"i"	"u"	"e"	"o"
as in father	as in ink	as in flute	as in end	as in oatmeal

A bar over a vowel means that the sound is long. Say *obāsan* (grandma), not *obasan* (aunt).

When you see vowel pairs: say **ie** as "ee-eh"; say **ee** as "eh-eh"; say **oo** as "o-oo"; say **ae** as "ah-eh"; say **ei** like the "ay" in "day"; say **ai** like Thai.

Other things you need to know

For other sounds, say them as you normally would, but with these tips in mind:

> **g** sounds like "g" in "go";
> **r** sounds more like "l";
> **fu** sounds halfway between "foo" and "hoo";
> **n** sound is a nasal "n" sound, said as if you had a stuffy nose;
> **(w)o** sound is shown with "w" in brackets because you write "wo", but say "o".

Stress

In Japanese, you say each part of a word with equal stress. Say e-da-ma-me, not e-da-MA-me.

Writing Japanese

Proper stroke order is from left to right and top to bottom. Normally, horizontal strokes are written before vertical strokes.

BONUS MATERIAL
Ever cut a hole in the side of a cereal box so you can get the prize at the bottom? Now you don't have to. Inside this book, the authors have created special BONUS MATERIAL designed to build your vocabulary. Can you find it?

About this book

This book is for everyone who is learning Japanese and for anyone who has an inquisitive brain.

The Japanese *kana* used in this book are the traditional sounds of Japanese, called *hiragana*. Don't worry. They're easy to learn. With this book's special **Triple Bubble Learning System**™, you'll learn *kana* quickly and easily. Just follow the simple steps below.

First, look at the pronunciation key and say the *kana* sound aloud. Then, look at the giant *kana* and say its sound three times as you trace it with your finger—this helps *kana* stick in your brain. Next, read the word next to the *kana*. Then, look for its picture or definition. Matching *kana* with words, pictures and definitions makes *kana* unforgettable, and it's fun.

Each page is specially designed with six user-friendly features:

1. **Giant *kana*** helps you fix its shape in your brain. Inside, stroke order arrows help you develop accurate style.

2. **Pronunciation key** teaches you to say each sound in a really Japanese way.

6. **Color-coding** for each *kana* set allows you to study *kana* together or separately.

3. **Japanese-English vocabulary** are linked with colorful illustrations; simple definitions make them easy to remember.

5. **Authentic descriptions** about Japanese culture and customs help you remember *kana* and increase your knowledge of Japan.

4. **Page numbers** in Japanese teach you how to count from 1 to 52.

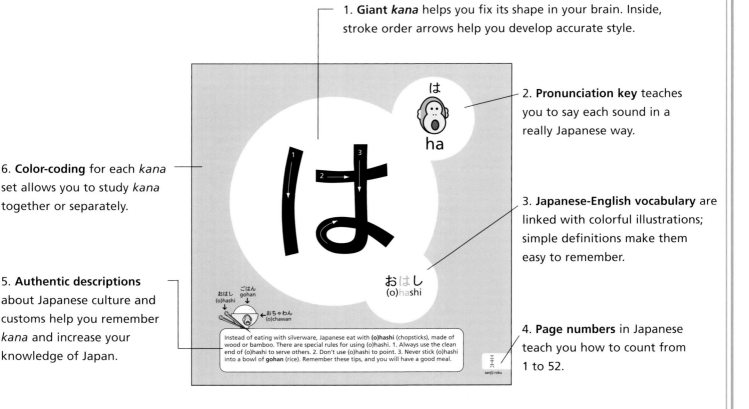

In the back, there's a word list with definitions, colorful numbers page, lively visual library and color-coded *hiragana* table. Use this material to quickly review what you've learned in this book.

About the characters

Learning the names and personalities of the characters will add to the fun you get from using this book. Each character plays a special role in teaching you Japanese.

Introducing:

Jimi

Jimi is an inquisitive, charming monkey who loves all things Japanese from anime to sushi. *Keitai denwa* (mobile phone) and a MD player are two gadgets he is never without. Born and raised in Tokyo, Jimi loves to play *gorufu* (golf), sing karaoke and eat *yakiniku* (Korean barbeque). His favorite food is peanut butter and boysenberry jelly sandwiches. Jimi's best pal is Robotto-san, a robot who loves to play the complex strategy game, *Go*.

In this book, Jimi not only instructs you on the finer points of the Japanese language, but also helps you build your vocabulary through full-color illustrations that detail everything from fruits and vegetables to parts of a person's body.

Robotto-san

With a T621-certified operating system, Robotto-san is a planetary authority on a variety of subjects, including Japanese. A native of Yokohama, Robotto-san spent many years with philosophers, monks and cultural experts around the universe before helping write this book. Espresso and herbal energy drinks keep his system tip-top. In his free time, Robotto-san enjoys Zen meditation and reading manga.

Watch for Robotto-san as he defines key vocabulary and explains significant cultural nuances in detail, so you can speak and act Japanese in real-life situations.

Akiko

Akiko is one of Jimi's closest (and most dramatic) friends. Nearly obsessed with fashion, Akiko spends most of her free time in Tokyo's Aoyama district shopping for the latest big-brand fashions along the Omotosando strip. She enjoys eating sashimi and drinking ocha with her many girlfriends.

In Japanese, there are many greetings for different situations and for different times of day. Keep an eye out for Akiko as she teaches you what greeting to say and when to say it.

さぁ　はじめよう
Let's Start!

あ

a

あたま
atama

← あたま
atama

← あし
ashi

↑
あご
ago

い
i

いけばな
ikebana

いけばな
ikebana

Ikebana is the traditional art of arranging flowers. A typical display is based on three lines that symbolize **shin** (heaven), **soe** (mankind) and **hikae** (Earth). Mastering ikebana requires three to five years of schooling and many, many years of practice.

う

u

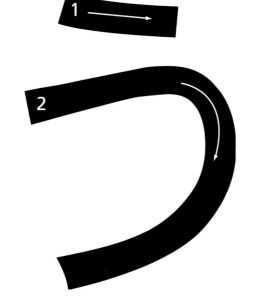

うなぎ
unagi

うなぎ
↙ unagi

Why do Japanese live so long? One reason: **unagi** (eel). Unagi is healthy and rich in protein, vitamins and minerals. **Unadon**, a popular unagi dish, is grilled eel seasoned with teriyaki sauce, served on a bed of rice. Finding an unagi shop is simple, just look for a sign with " う " in the shape of an eel.

え

e

1 →

2

えど
edo

 うきよえ
ukiyo-e

The **Edo** period (1603-1868) is one of the greatest periods in Japanese art history. In this time, artists thrived and created inspiring works of art including sculpture, decorative screens, **ukiyo-e** paintings and ikebana. For Japanese, the Edo period represents nearly everything that is traditional Japanese culture.

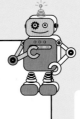

お

o

1 → 2 ↓ 3 →

おじぎ
ojigi

おじぎ
ojigi
↘

Ojigi (bowing) is an important custom in Japan. Instead of shaking hands, Japanese bow. It is a way to show respect and to say "hello" and "thank you." To bow, bend at your waist, hands at your sides. It is impolite not to return a bow. It might feel strange to ojigi, but when you do, you will be considered polite.

か

ka

かみのけ
kaminoke

かみのけ
kaminoke

かた
kata

かかと
kakato

き

ki

きもの
kimono

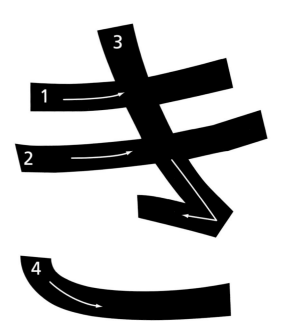

きもの
kimono

Kimono is the native costume of Japan worn by men, women and children. Dressing in kimono is no casual matter. A woman's kimono is quite elaborate and colorful. Usually made of fine silk, it is hand-sewn and very expensive. A kimono is worn with an **obi**, a belt made of silk in a contrasting color.

く

ku

くち
kuchi

← くち
kuchi

← くちびる
kuchibiru

← くび
kubi

け

ke

けいたい
keitai

けいたい
keitai ↓

もしもし
mo shi mo shi

For many Japanese, **keitai denwa** (mobile phone) is the preferred form of communication. With keitai, you can send email, browse the Web and download ring tones. When in public places, it is polite to switch your keitai to "manners mode" and use it in special areas only. When you answer a keitai say "**Moshi-moshi**" (hello).

こ

ko

こんにちは
konnichiwa

こんにちは
konnichiwa

When you greet someone in Japan, you say a greeting depending on time of day. In the morning, say "**Ohayō**" (good morning). In the afternoon, say "**Konnichiwa**" (good afternoon). In the evening, say "**Konbanwa**" (good evening). If you say these greetings, you will make many friends.

さ

sa

さしみ
sashimi

さしみ
sashimi

Sashimi is thinly sliced, fresh, raw fish flavored with **wasabi** (horseradish) and **shōyu** (soy sauce). It is like **sushi**, except there is no rice. There are many types of sashimi: **tako** (octopus), **awabi** (abalone), **hamachi** (yellow tail), **ika** (squid) and **maguro** (tuna). Sashimi is delicious and a great source of protein.

し
shi

1

しんかんせん
shinkansen

しんかんせん
shinkansen

The world famous **Shinkansen** (bullet train) runs from Tokyo to Fukuoka at speeds of more than 175 km/h. On it, there is a first-class car, vending machines, telephones— even a snack and gift cart that comes up and down the aisle. Buy a ticket for the Shinkansen at the **kippu uriba** (ticket office).

す

su

すし
sushi

すし
sushi

In the 7th century, China introduced **sushi** to Japan. To make it, raw seafood is placed on top of sticky white rice seasoned with vinegar. Some sushi are wrapped with **nori** (dried seaweed). There are many types of sushi including **nigiri-zushi** (finger rolls) and **maki-zushi** (hand rolls). Sushi is low in fat and highly nutritious.

せ

se

せんせい
sensei

せんせい
sensei

おんなのこ
onnanoko

おとこのこ
otokonoko

In Japan, it is impolite to call a person by name. Instead, you add **san** to a name or title to show respect. For example, the proper way to refer to Mr. Yamada is "Yamada-san." Professor Junko is "Junko-san" or "Junko Sensei." Remember, it is important to be humble and courteous while in Japan.

そ

SO

そば
soba

そば
soba

Soba is a thin, brown noodle made from buckwheat flour. There are many ways to eat soba. You can eat it hot or cold, flavored with shōyu or topped with vegetables and tempura. Soba is full of vitamins and minerals. If you eat soba on December 31, you will live life well in the new year.

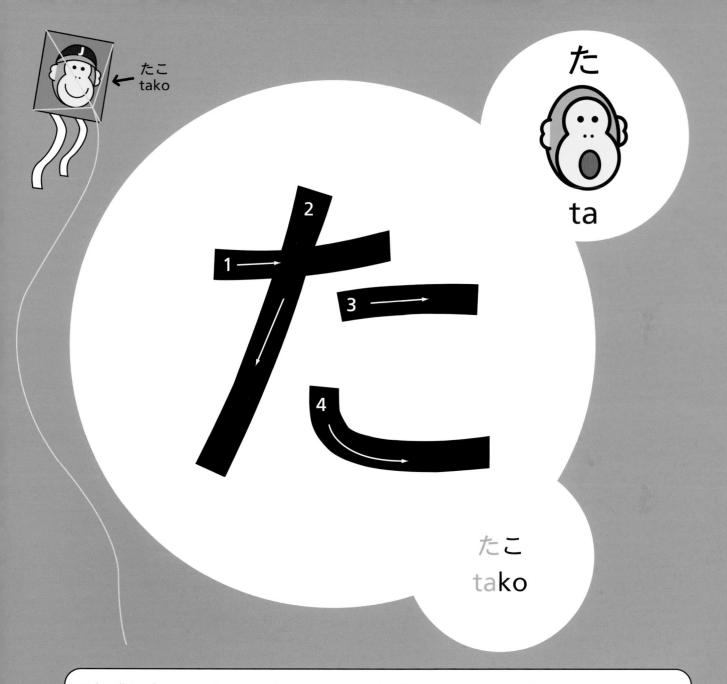

たこ
tako

た
ta

たこ
tako

Tako (kites) originally were flown as part of religious ceremonies to make special requests of gods and spirits. Tako are made of a bamboo or wood frame and special paper painted with colorful designs and bold patterns. The most popular tako designs depict Japanese **samurai** (warriors), **kami** (gods) and **semi** (cicada).

ち

chi

もち
mochi

もち
mochi

On New Year's Day, every Japanese family eats **mochi**, a sweet rice cake. Mochi also is eaten during Shinto festivals and weddings. It is said that eating mochi provides nourishment for your soul. Mochi is eaten plain or with **anko** (sweet red beans), nori or shōyu. Got mochi?

つ

tsu

1

つる

tsuru

つる
tsuru

Origami is the art of folding a single sheet of paper in special ways to create different shapes. The most popular shape is a **tsuru** (crane). Origami has existed since the 6th century, when **kami** (paper) was introduced to Japan. Back then, paper was folded to make decorations for religious ceremonies.

て

te

1

おてら
(o)tera

ぶつぞう →
butsu-zō

Japan has two main religions: Shinto and Buddhism. Many Japanese follow both. There are thousands of Buddhist (o)tera (temples) and Shinto **jinja** (shrines) around Tokyo. Asakusa Sensō-ji and Meiji-Jingū are two of the most famous. When you visit (o)tera, be sure to pay your respects to **butsu-zō** and your wishes may come true.

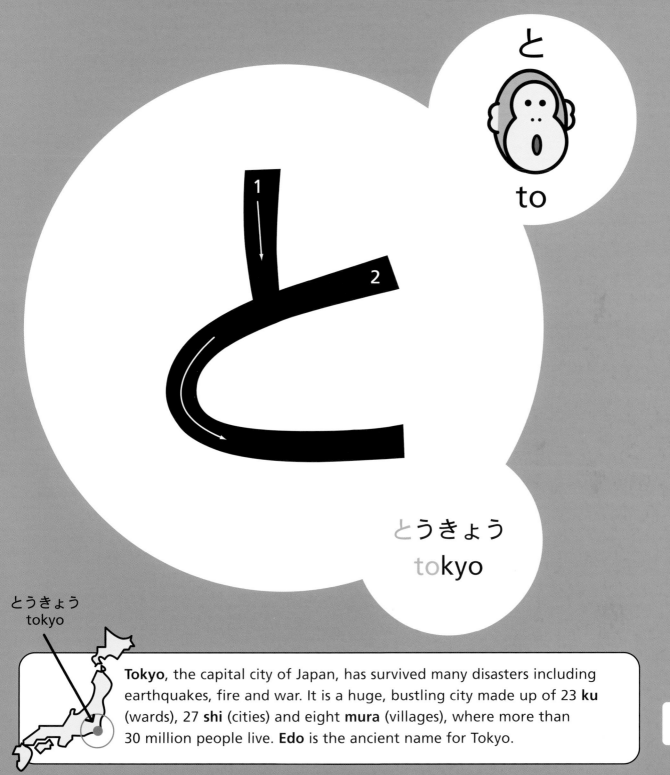

と

to

とうきょう
tokyo

とうきょう
tokyo

Tokyo, the capital city of Japan, has survived many disasters including earthquakes, fire and war. It is a huge, bustling city made up of 23 **ku** (wards), 27 **shi** (cities) and eight **mura** (villages), where more than 30 million people live. **Edo** is the ancient name for Tokyo.

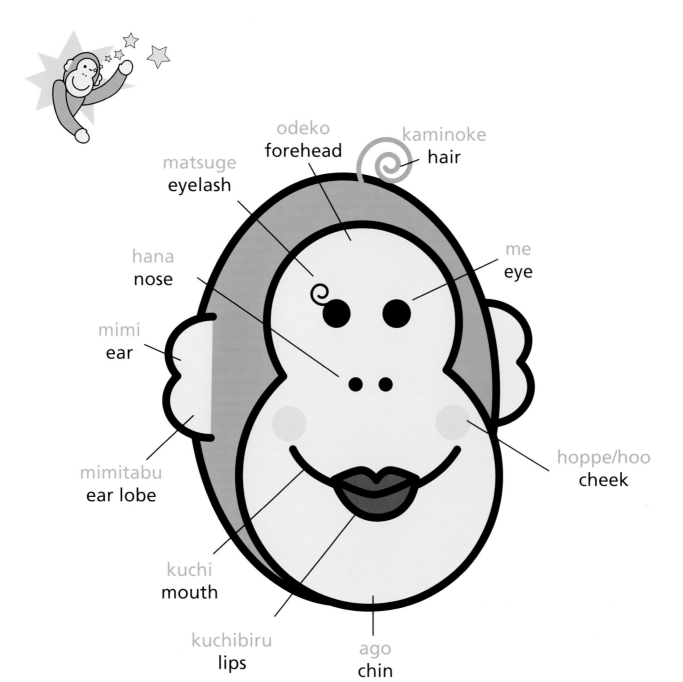

matsuge
eyelash

odeko
forehead

kaminoke
hair

hana
nose

me
eye

mimi
ear

mimitabu
ear lobe

hoppe/hoo
cheek

kuchi
mouth

kuchibiru
lips

ago
chin

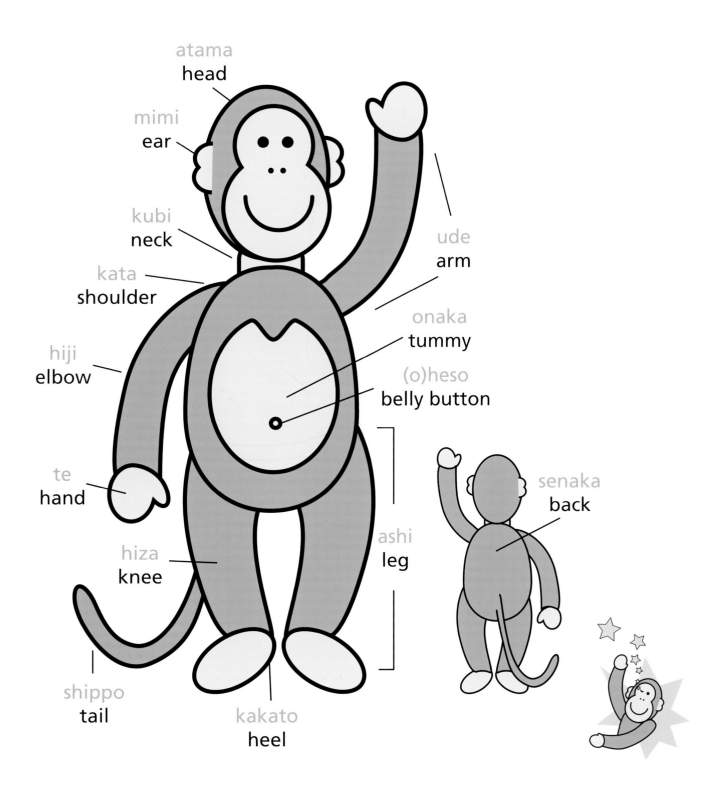

atama
head

mimi
ear

kubi
neck

kata
shoulder

hiji
elbow

te
hand

hiza
knee

shippo
tail

kakato
heel

ude
arm

onaka
tummy

(o)heso
belly button

ashi
leg

senaka
back

な
na

1 2 3 4

な

なし
nashi

なし nashi

ようなし yōnashi

なす nasu

に

ni

にほん
nihon

ひのまる
hinomaru

The Land of the Rising Sun, **Nihon** (Japan), is a volcanic island chain located in Eastern Asia between the North Pacific Ocean and the Sea of Japan. It is slightly smaller in size than California, with a population of more than 126 million people. In Nihon, **Nihon-jin** (Japanese people) speak **Nihon-go** (Japanese).

ぬ

nu

ぬりえ
nurie

ぬりえ
nurie →

くれよん
kureyon ↓

ね

ne

ねこ
neko

まねきねこ
maneki neko

Japanese adore good luck charms. One famous lucky charm is **Maneki Neko**, a gesturing cat that is placed in a store or restaurant to attract customers and bring good luck. Tradition says that the left paw invites customers in, and the right paw welcomes good fortune: "Money come, money come."

の

no

のう
nō

のうめん
nōmen

Nō is ancient Japanese theater that combines dance, drama, music and poetry. There are two types of Nō stories: reality and dreams. In dreams, actors portray ghosts, gods and demons. In both, actors wear colorful masks and speak in a unique tone. Music for the stories is played by **hayashi** (orchestra).

は

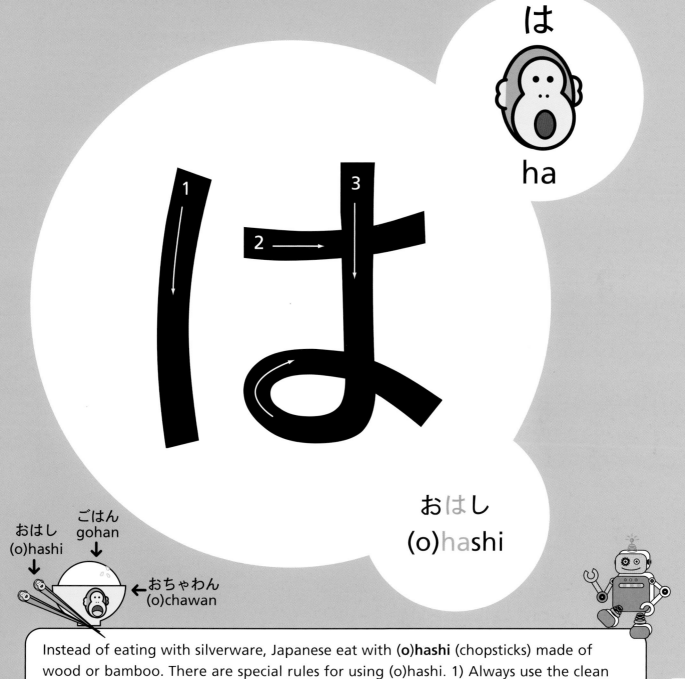

ha

おはし
(o)hashi

おはし
(o)hashi

ごはん
gohan

おちゃわん
(o)chawan

Instead of eating with silverware, Japanese eat with **(o)hashi** (chopsticks) made of wood or bamboo. There are special rules for using (o)hashi. 1) Always use the clean end of (o)hashi to serve others. 2) Don't use (o)hashi to point. 3) Never stick (o)hashi into a bowl of **gohan** (rice). Remember these tips, and you will have a good meal.

ひ

hi

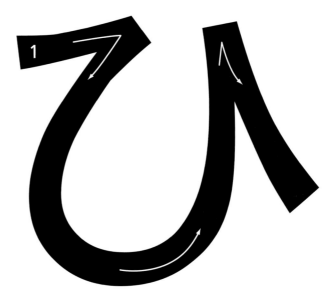

ひらがな
hiragana

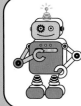

In this book you are learning **hiragana**, signs used for traditional sounds of Japanese. Once you master hiragana, you will learn **katakana**. Katakana signs are used for words that Japanese has borrowed from other languages. What is the secret to learning Japanese? Practice. Practice. Practice!

ふぐ
fugu

ふ
fu

ふとん
futon

まくら
makura

ふとん
futon

Most Japanese sleep on a **futon**, a thin mattress with thick quilts and a **makura** (pillow) placed on **tatami** (straw mats). In the morning, the futon is neatly folded and placed in **oshiire** (closet) so the room can return to normal use. Sleeping on futon is good for your back, and it is fun.

へ
he

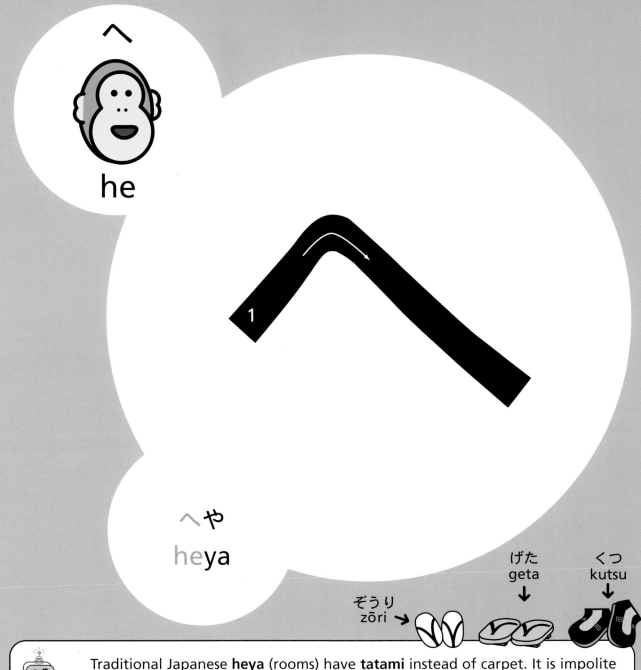

1

へや
heya

ぞうり
zōri →

げた
geta
↓

くつ
kutsu
↓

Traditional Japanese **heya** (rooms) have **tatami** instead of carpet. It is impolite to walk on tatami with your shoes. Always remove your shoes at the front door whenever you enter a Japanese house. If you remember this, you will be invited again.

ほ
ho

ほうりゅうじ
horyuji

ほうりゅうじ
horyuji
ごじゅうのとう
gojū no tō

Horyuji is a historic Buddhist temple in Nara, Japan. Founded in 607 by Prince Shotoku and Empress Suiko, it is home to over 1,700 treasures of Buddhist art and architecture. Horyuji is divided into two sections: **higashi** (east) and **nishi** (west). The higashi temple contains the world's oldest building and a five-story pagoda.

ま

ma

まんが
manga

まんが
manga
↓

Comic books, cartoons and comic strips are called **manga**. Manga is a wildly popular form of art and entertainment in Japan. Tezuka Osamu, is the best known manga artist. During his career, he created more than 700 stories and 170,000 manga pieces. One of his most famous characters is Astro Boy, a robot with a warm heart.

Astro Boy, TM & ©Tezuka Production Corporation

み
mi

すみません
sumimasen

すみません
sumimasen

Sumimasen is a simple and useful expression you can use in many situations. If you step on someone's toe, say "Sumimasen." If you want to say sorry, say "Sumimasen." If you want to say "Excuse me," guess what you say? "Sumimasen!" *Sumimasen... you may turn the page...*

む

mu

さむらい

samurai

かたな
katana

さむらい
samurai →

Samurai were the elite military class during the **Edo** period. A samurai was expected to be loyal to his **Shogun** (master), no matter what the personal consequences of his duty. **Rōnin** was a samurai who lost his status due to misdeeds or the untimely death of his Shogun. **Katana** (sword) was the mark of a samurai.

め
me

め
me

め
me

めがね
megane

めぐすり
megusuri

も

mo

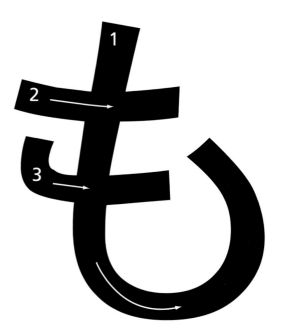

1
2 →
3 →

すもう

sumo

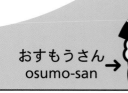

じみ錦

おすもうさん →
osumo-san

Sumo (wrestling) is the national sport of Japan. Two **osumo-san** (wrestlers) fight in a **dohyō** (ring). Each tries to defeat his opponent by using a combination of pushes, holds and throws. The first to make his opponent touch the ground with his body or step outside of the dohyō wins.

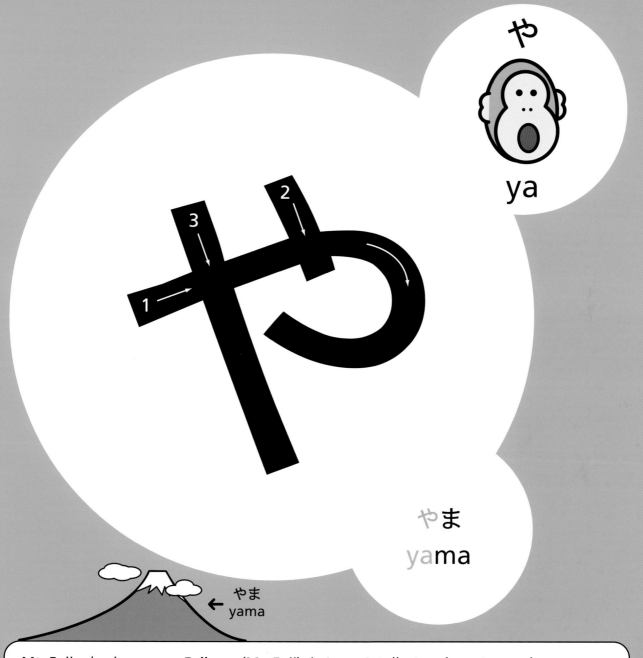

や
ya

やま
yama

← やま
yama

Mt. Fuji, also known as **Fuji-san** (Mr. Fuji), is Japan's tallest and most sacred **yama** (mountain). Standing 3,376 meters high, many Japanese dream of climbing Fuji-san at least once in their life. In summer, people climb to the top of Mt. Fuji to worship **kami** (gods).

ゆ

yu

ゆのみ
yunomi

おちゃ
ocha

ゆのみ
yunomi

Ocha (green tea) is the most popular drink in Japan. To make it, tea leaves are placed in a **kyūsu** (teapot) and boiled water is poured on top. Next, it's poured in a **yunomi**, a cup with no handles. When you visit someone's home you will be offered ocha. It is impolite not to accept, even if you don't drink ocha.

よ
yo

2
1

よこづな
yokozuna

← よこづな
yokozuna

Sumo are ranked by skill, not weight. There are ten grades of sumo from **jonokuchi** (novice) to **yokozuna** (expert). Promotion to yokozuna requires skill, a winning record and sound moral character. Reaching yokozuna is no easy task. Over the last 300 years, only 70 have reached this level.

ら

ra

らーめん
ramen

らーめん
ramen

Oodles of Chinese noodles, bowls, soup utensils and **ramen** adverts are on display at the **Shin-Yokohama Ramen Museum**. Here, you can view ramen's 600-year history, from the samurai who loved it to the world's first instant ramen. There's even a theme park, **Ramen Town**, where you can sample tasty ramen from all over Japan.

り
ri

りんご
ringo

りんご
ringo

りんごじゅーす
ringo jūsu

りんごあめ
ringo ame

る

ru

はる
haru

さくら
sakura

Haru (spring) is when Japan celebrates its national flower, **sakura** (cherry blossom), with **Hanami** (cherry blossom viewing) parties. It is a time to sing, dance, write poems and eat special foods. Hanami is many centuries old and was originally enjoyed by wealthy Japanese. Today, everyone enjoys Hanami.

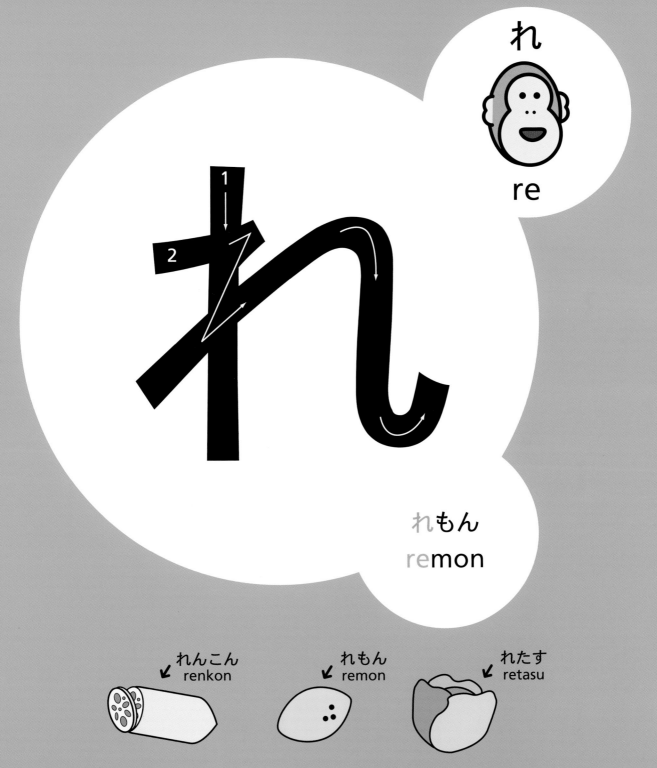

れ
re

れもん
remon

れんこん
renkon

れもん
remon

れたす
retasu

ろ

ro

ろぼっと さん
robotto-san

ろぼっと さん
robotto-san

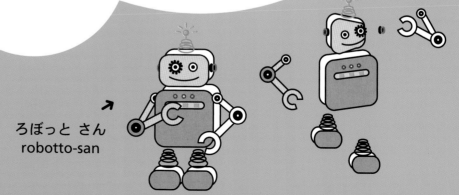

わ

wa

わし
washi

↖ ちょうちん
chōchin

Washi, a special paper made from Japanese tree bark, is known for its strength, decorative color and creative designs. In ancient times, washi was prized for writing poetry and diaries. Today, washi is used for many things including stationery, fans, dolls, **chōchin** (lanterns) and **shōji** (screens).

を

WO

を
(w)o

ん
n

ん

じみーちゃん
jimī-chan

じみー
jimī

のんき
nonki

うれしい
ureshii

かなしい
kanashii

おなかがすいた
onaka ga suita

おこった
okotta

だめ!

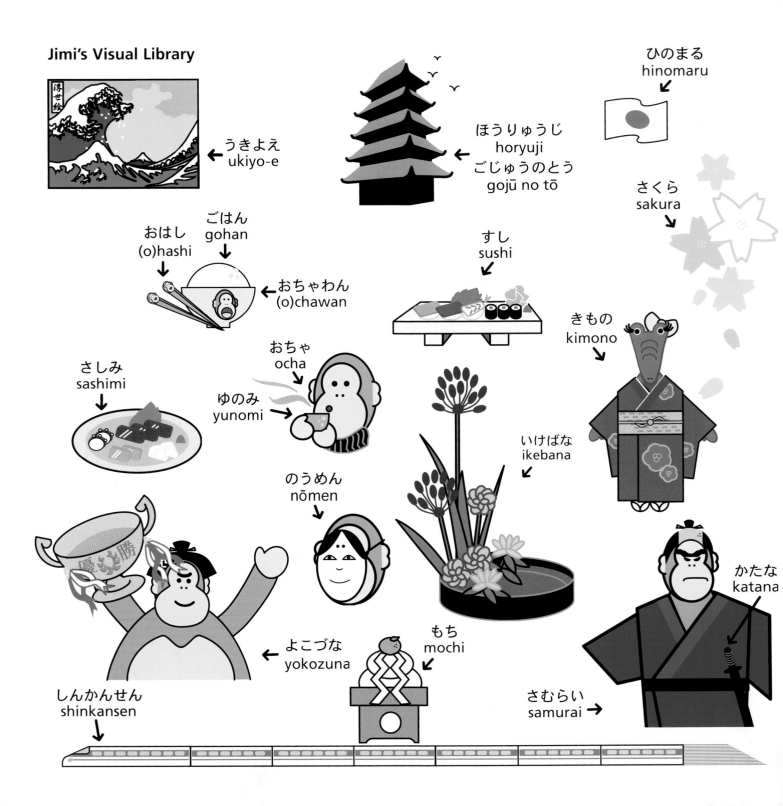

Jimi's Visual Library

うきよえ
ukiyo-e

ほうりゅうじ
horyuji
ごじゅうのとう
gojū no tō

ひのまる
hinomaru

さくら
sakura

おはし
(o)hashi

ごはん
gohan

おちゃわん
(o)chawan

すし
sushi

きもの
kimono

さしみ
sashimi

おちゃ
ocha

ゆのみ
yunomi

いけばな
ikebana

のうめん
nōmen

かたな
katana

よこづな
yokozuna

もち
mochi

しんかんせん
shinkansen

さむらい
samurai →

おなかがすいた
onaka ga suita

らーめん
ramen

ちょうちん
chōchin

じみー
jimī

あきこ
akiko

ろぼっと さん
robotto-san

かた
kata

れたす
retasu

のんき
nonki

りんご
ringo

かなしい
kanashii

おこった
okotta

だめ!

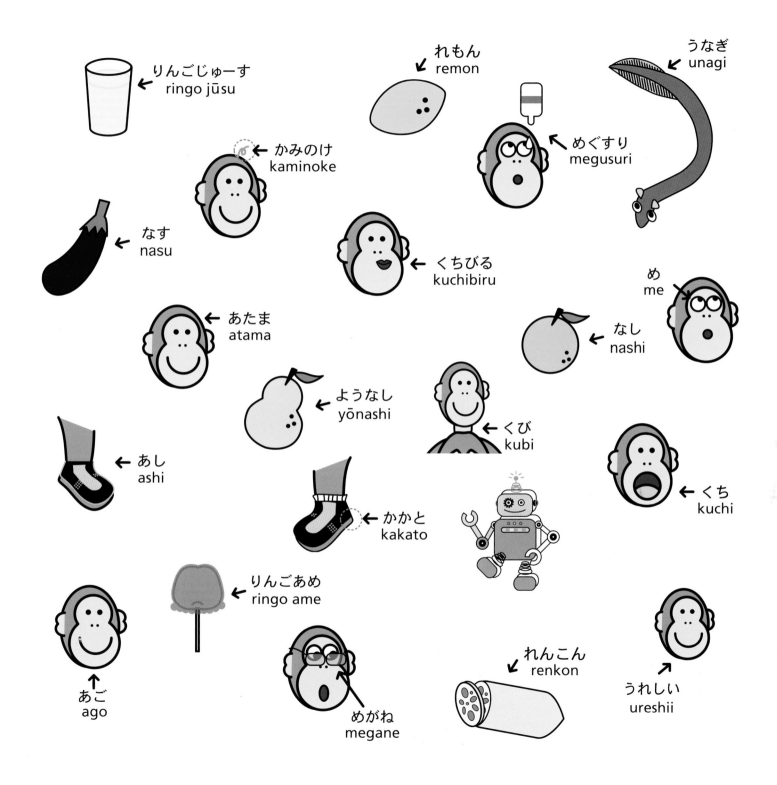

Numbers

一   ichi

二   ni

三   san

四   shi/yon

五   go

六   roku

七   nana/shichi

八   hachi

九   kyū/ku

十   jū

Word List

A
ago — chin
anko — sweet bean paste
arigatō — Thank you!
ashi — paw; foot; leg
atama — head; face
awabi — abalone

B
butsu-zō — Buddha statue

C
chawan — rice bowl
chōchin — lantern

D
dohyō — sumo ring

E
edo — Tokyo (ancient)

F
futon — a thin mattress; bedding

G
geta — traditional wooden clogs
gohan — rice (cooked); meal
gojū no tō — five-story pagoda
gorufu — golf

H
hamachi — yellow tail
hanami — cherry blossom viewing
haru — spring
hashi — chopsticks
hayashi — orchestra for a Nō play
(o)heso — belly button
heya — room
higashi — east
hiji — elbow
hikae — Earth
hinomaru — Japanese flag
hiragana — signs used for traditional sounds of Japanese
hiza — knee
ho/hoppe — cheek
horyuji — a historic Buddhist temple (607) in Nara, Japan

I
ika — squid
ikebana — flower arrangement

J
jinja — Shinto shrine(s)

K
kakato — heel; foot
kami — god(s); hair
kaminoke — hair (single)
kanashii — sad
kata — shoulder
katakana — signs used for words from other languages
keitai denwa — mobile phone

	kimono	traditional Japanese dress
	kippu uriba	ticket office
	konbanwa	Good evening!
	konnichiwa	Good afternoon!
	kubi	neck
	kuchi	mouth
	kuchibiru	lips
	kureyon	crayon
	kutsu	shoes
	kyūsu	tea pot
M	maguro	tuna
	maki-zushi	rolled sushi
	makura	pillow
	maneki neko	good luck kitty icon
	manga	comic books; cartoons; comic strips
	matsuge	eyelash
	me	eye(s)
	megane	eye glasses
	megusuri	eye drops
	mimi	ear
	mimitabu	ear lobe
	mochi	sweet rice cake
	moshi-moshi	Hello. (phone)
N	nashi	Asian pear
	nasu	eggplant
	neko	cat
	nihon	Japan
	nihongo	Japanese language
	nihonjin	Japanese person/people
	nigiri-zushi	finger roll
	nishi	west
	Nō	ancient Japanese theatre
	nōmen	Nō mask
	nonki	happy-go-lucky
	nori	dried seaweed
	nurie	coloring
O	obi	silk sash for kimono
	ocha	green tea
	odeko	forehead
	ohayō	Good morning!
	ojigi	bowing
	okotta	angry
	onaka	tummy
	onaka ga suita	hungry
	origami	art of folding a single sheet of paper
	oshiire	futon closet
R	ramen	Chinese-style noodles
	remon	lemon
	renkon	lotus root

	retasu	lettuce
	ringo	apple
	ringo ame	candied apple
	ringo jūsu	apple juice
	rōnin	masterless samurai
S	sakura	cherry blossom; cherry tree
	samurai	elite military class during Edo period; Japanese warrior
	–san	Mr., Mrs., Ms.; added title to show respect
	sashimi	sliced fresh raw fish
	sayōnara	Goodbye!
	senaka	back
	sensei	teacher, professor; master
	shiawase	happy
	shin	heaven
	shinkansen	bullet train
	Shinto	official Japanese religion
	shippo	tail
	Shogun	samurai master
	shōji	screen
	shōyu	soy sauce
	soba	thin buckwheat noodle
	soe	mankind
	sumimasen	Excuse me! I'm sorry!
	sumo	Japan's national sport, wrestling
	(o)sumo-san	sumo wrestler
	sushi	rice seasoned with vinegar, topped with fish or vegetables
T	tako	octopus; kite
	tatami	straw mat
	tempura	deep-fried, battered vegetable or seafood
	tera	Buddhist temple
	Tokyo	capital city of Japan
	tsuru	crane
U	ude	arm
	udon	thick wheat noodle
	ukiyo-e	traditional Japanese wood block print
	unadon	grilled eel seasoned with teriyaki sauce, on a bed of rice
	unagi	eel
W	wasabi	Japanese horseradish
	washi	Japanese paper
Y	yakiniku	Korean barbeque
	yama	mountain
	yokozuna	Grand Champion; highest sumo rank
	yōnashi	pear
	yunomi	tea cup
Z	zōri	traditional sandals

Hiragana Chart

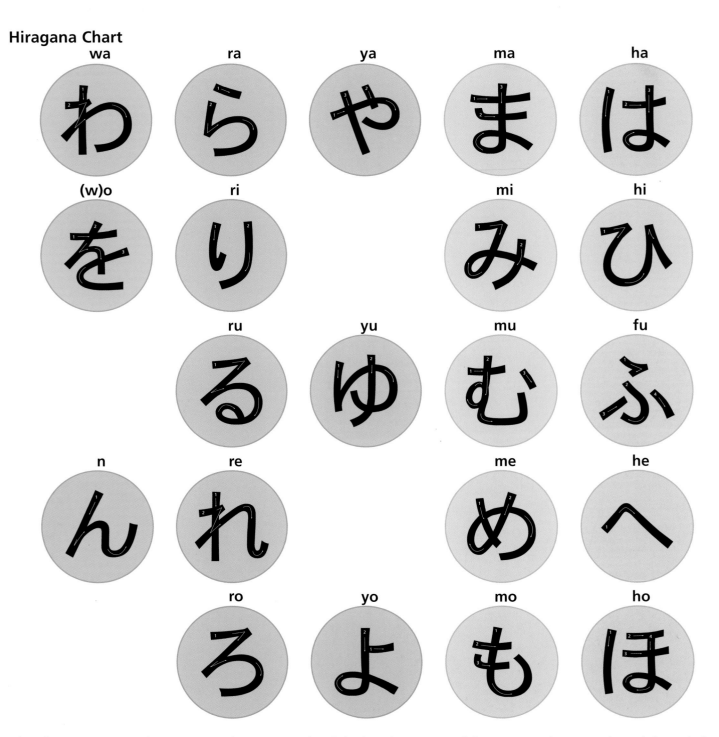

This chart is presented Japanese-style. Start on the right-hand page. Read from top to bottom, then right to left.
NOTE: The syllables **yi**, **ye**, **wi**, **wu** and **we** do not exist in modern Japanese.

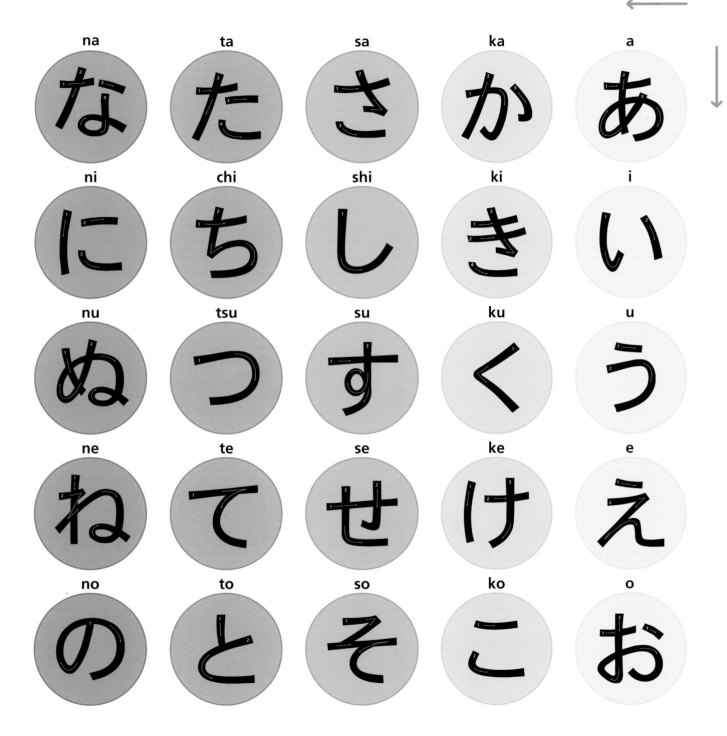

ありがとう
arigatō!

Publisher's acknowledgements
I am grateful and lucky to be here to work with
Peter and Yumie. I wish you both great success. This thank you
is for future as well as past efforts.

Authors' acknowledgements
To my family, thank you for being interested and supportive through the years.
Special thanks to Yumie. Thanks also to Junko-sensei, Katherine Buttler, David
Butler, Kathleeen O'Brien, Matt McClendon, Andy V. and 10K Tod. Also, thanks
to Carol Klohn, and Auntie Elma's for giving me my start in a foreign language.
— Peter X. Takahashi

• • •

I am grateful to have the opportunity to compile, design and illustrate
this book on Japanese. Special thanks to Andrew and Isaac for their
thoughtful, creative guidance. Also, thanks to my family, Mako-chan,
Sylvia Nielsen, Matt McClendon, Junko-sensei, Katherine Buttler,
Jody Mihelic, Daniel Wong. Many, many thanks to
Peter for his tremendous efforts.
— Yumie Toka

ピーター X.
peter x.

ゆみえ
yumie

Peter X. Takahashi is a writer, publisher, marketer, creative strategy consultant—and sometimes karaoke king—who recently escaped the elbow-smashing world of an enormously sterile corporate existence. This is his first book. He lives and works in Atlanta.

Yumie Toka is an award-winning designer and illustrator whose work is enjoyed internationally by kids, adults, and colleagues alike. This is her first book. In her free time she enjoys spending time with her two boys perfecting the "Jimi Roll"—an eclectic sushi roll based on the main character in this book. She lives and works in Atlanta.

Check out **www.pbjomnimedia.com** for additional tips on Japanese, updates, special BONUS MATERIAL, future products, and MORE. Prepare your brain for nourishment...